W9-AFG-813

www.brookscole.com

www.brookscole.com is the World Wide Web site for Thomson Brooks/Cole and is your direct source to dozens of online resources.

At *www.brookscole.com* you can find out about supplements, demonstration software, and student resources. You can also send email to many of our authors and preview new publications and exciting new technologies.

www.brookscole.com
Changing the way the world learns®

Primer for Critiquing Social Research

A Student Guide

Michael J. Holosko
University of Windsor
Ontario, Canada

THOMSON
BROOKS/COLE

Australia • Brazil • Canada • Mexico • Singapore • Spain • United Kingdom • United States

THOMSON

BROOKS/COLE

Executive Editor: *Lisa Gebo*
Acquisitions Editor: *Marquita Flemming*
Assistant Editor: *Monica Arvin*
Editorial Assistant: *Christine Northup*
Technology Project Manager: *Darin Derstine*
Marketing Manager: *Caroline Concilla*
Marketing Assistant: *Rebecca Weisman*

Advertising Project Manager: *Tami Strang*
Project Manager, Editorial Production: *Christy Krueger*
Print Buyer: *Barbara Britton*
Permissions Editor: *Sarah Harkrader*
Cover Designer: *Ross Carron*
Printer: *Webcom*

Printed in Canada
2 3 4 5 6 7   09 08 07 06 05

For more information about our products,
contact us at:
**Thomson Learning Academic Resource
Center
1-800-423-0563**

For permission to use material from this
text or product, submit a request online at
http://www.thomsonrights.com
Any additional questions about permissions
can be submitted by email at
thomsonrights@thomson.com

Thomson Higher Education
10 Davis Drive
Belmont, CA 94002-3098
USA

Library of Congress Control Number:
2005929199

ISBN 0-495-00774-9

Table of Contents

About the Author

Preface

Acknowledgements

Chapter 1 Introduction to a Primer for Critiquing Social Research: A Student Guide

Chapter 2 Science or Not? Research or Not? Science and Research

Chapter 3 Qualitative vs. Quantitative Research

Chapter 4 Writing Clarity, Title, Author's Affiliation, Abstract, and References

Chapter 5 The Three Main Content Areas of the Quantitative Research Article: Introduction, Method, and Results

Chapter 10 Concluding Remarks

List of Figures

List of Boxes

List of Tables

About the Author

MICHAEL J. HOLOSKO, PhD, MSW, is a professor of social work at the University of Windsor and adjunct instructor at Norfolk State University. He has taught in schools of social work (primarily), nursing, public administration, and applied social science in Canada, the United States, Hong Kong, Australia, and the U.S. Virgin Islands. For the past 26 years, he has been a consultant to a variety of large and small health and human service organizations in the areas of program evaluation, outcomes, organizational development, communication, leadership, visioning, organizational alignment, and stress management. He has published numerous monographs, chapters, articles, and texts in the areas of evaluation, health care, gerontology, social policy, music intervention, and spirituality. He is on the editorial boards of Research on Social Work Practice; the Journal of Social Service Research; the Journal of Health and Social Policy; Stress, Trauma, and Crisis; the Journal of Human Behavior and Social Environment; the Hong Kong Journal of Social Work; and the Journal of Evidence-Based Social Work Practice. He has served on numerous boards of directors for a variety of local, provincial, federal, and international human service agencies, including Health and Welfare, Canada's Research Advisory Committee. Over the past few years he has taken his concerns for advocacy and social justice to the airwaves, where he is billed as "The Community Doctor" on AM800 CKLW and The New WI out of Windsor, Ontario, Canada.

Preface

This text was written at the request of numerous undergraduate and graduate students in the social sciences and helping professions who wanted a simple, "hands-on" way to critique social research. Over the past 26 years of teaching statistics, quantitative, qualitative, and evaluation research in schools of social work, nursing, public administration, and medicine, I observed that students routinely critique, assess, and appraise articles, studies, and research reports in their respective fields of study for a variety of reasons (e.g., for class assignments, to appraise and acquire knowledge, and/or to develop critical or analytic thinking skills). Whatever the reason, having a critiquing template or analytic tool to achieve this purpose seems both necessary and relevant for any student who wishes to make an informed assessment of the research study they are critiquing.

This text is conceptualized and written as a primer for students for the following reasons. First, there are numerous weighty "research methods" texts written in a variety of disciplines. These basically inform students about "everything they wanted to know about research in their respective field of study—-but were afraid to ask." So another methods text this is not. Instead, this text is designed to supplement other research texts that are written about methodology, statistics, design, or the like. Second, it is purposely written in a more casual and (hopefully) user-friendly voice, in order to share candid insights about social research and "the story behind the study" you are critiquing or assessing.

Third, the criteria presented herein to critique both quantitative and qualitative social research are presented as minimal criteria. Thus, students and teachers may choose to add to these as they see fit.

Finally, it is called a primer and student guide because it offers information for further discussion. Its use will hopefully trigger and promote the critical thinking and analytic skills of students and teachers alike. A critique template can be found on the book companion website at http://counseling.wadsworth.com/Holosko1e for evaluating downloaded articles will be offered in conjunction with the text for students, teachers, or other research consumers to share information about the primer and its use.

Acknowledgements

In a Zen-like way, we are today what our life experiences have shaped us to be. Therefore, I would like to acknowledge five different support groups which have influenced my own personal and professional thinking about social research. The culmination and blending of these cohorts were indeed the real story behind this work. Cohort 1 is made up of those influential social work researchers/educators whose overt efforts pushed forward the agenda of empirically based practice, and enhanced research and evaluative thinking in our profession. They include M. Richmond, H. Bartlett, R. Cloward, E. Herzog, E. Greenwood, T. Tripodi, N. Polansky, E. Suchman, E. Thomas, J. Fischer, M. Bloom, W. Hudson, A. Rubin, R. Grinnell Jr., H. Goldstein, W. Reid, W. Epstein, E. Gambrill, L. Rutman, J. Wodarski, B. Thyer, and D. Padgett. Cohort 2 is the thousands of students whom I have taught social research to over the past 26 years—-thank you for your questions, insights, and making me listen to your research anxiety and concerns. My friends and colleagues who prodded, persuaded, and kept me focused on this project: D. Leslie, M. Feit, E. Risler, A. Sallee, B. Thyer, thank you. The fourth cohort includes publishers E. Bowers, M. Strawbridge, and M. Flemming, as well as reviewers L. Nackerud, University of Georgia; C. Dulmus, University of Tennessee; M. Feit, Norfolk State University; E. Au Lui, City University of Hong Kong; and V. Giannetti, Duquesne University. Thank you for believing in this endeavor from beginning to end. Finally, to my wife Ann, my consummate friend, partner, learner, and reality-check: thank you for your love, friendship, support, student voice, and simplifying both my life and thoughts.

M.J.H.

1

Introduction to A Primer for Critiquing Social Research: A Student Guide

Everything should be as simple as it is, but not simpler.
– A. Einstein

Introduction

This primer, or handbook, was written at the request of numerous undergraduate and graduate students who, over my 26 years of teaching, have taught me more about social research than I ever taught them. It provides a simple "hands-on" and straightforward approach to enable students to pick up any social research study and critique or assess it in an informed and intelligent way.

This text basically takes each section and subsection of a social research study and presents criteria that can be used to critique that respective section. In a step-by-step fashion, then, students can either assess the entire study or various parts of it, as they read through it with a critical eye. This primer is founded on a number of assumptions about social research that require tabling, as they underpin how the text was both conceptualized and written.

Assumptions About the Text

Critiquing is Step 1 to critical thinking. Critical thinking skills involve more than simply critiquing or assessing. They are founded upon first developing basic skills in critical appraisal. I have noted that when students or consumers of research develop some confidence in their abilities to critically appraise social research, they find themselves in a more favorable position to then develop their analytic and next level critical thinking skills.

You don't necessarily have to do research to understand it. In teaching social research in various social and behavioral sciences and helping professions, I have observed a myth that says, "The only way you can learn about research is to do it!" This is simply not the case. In fact, I have seen many students become even more confused and anxious about research when they were ill-prepared and then tossed into a research trial-by-fire experience. An informed and astute student of research with good critiquing skills holds the keys to important research knowledge, values, and skills: all of which can be further developed on one's research learning curve.

Research is not mysterious. I realize that for some, the terms research, science, statistics, hypothesis testing, etc., are anxiety provoking. I contend that this is mostly due to how these subjects are taught--not because they are either complex or mysterious. In this text, I try to demystify the subject of social research and present material in simple and concise ways in order to offset these unnecessary mysterious notions.

Although criteria are minimal, they are comprehensive. The various criteria presented herein which enable students to critique social research studies are deemed as minimal criteria. They reflect the "bare bones," or basics, of what should be included in a respective section or subsection of the research study you are critiquing. Certainly, other criteria may be added to these, and both students and teachers are encouraged to do so. However, this does not mean that just because they are minimal, they are not comprehensive. Each has been well researched and deemed important--or else they wouldn't have been included at all.

Just who is the target audience? I wrote this text and field-tested its contents over the years primarily for undergraduate students. This is not to say that graduate students or practitioners could not benefit from its use. Also, since I am a social work educator, the majority of case examples used within are drawn from my own discipline. The critiquing material, however, is interdisciplinary in nature, as basically social research is social research, regardless of who is conducting it. Thus, individuals from any social or behavioral science field or helping professionals who conduct social research can use this text to effectively critique research studies.

This is not another "research methods" text. This is not another so-called research methods text, which typically instructs students about how to conduct social research. The content is deliberately presented in a relatively non-judgemental way (I tried hard here), consciously avoiding instructing students about how to do research. Quite simply, this text is solely about critiquing social research. As such, it serves to supplement or complement other research methods texts.

Just what is being critiqued? This text allows students to critique various published research reports, studies, and articles. Since the target group is primarily students, the majority of research studies that they will likely read will appear in peer-reviewed professional scientific journals found in the library or on-line. The term research study then, for many, will mean the research study in the journal where you found it.

The APA format sets the stylistic requirements for the text. Since approximately 85-90% of the professional journals, reports, and studies cited in the social and behavioral sciences in North America use the American Psychological Association's (APA) stylistic requirements, this text uses them as the framework for critiquing the various components of a research study. These are set out in the Publication Manual of the American Psychological Association, 5th Edition (2001), Washington, DC: American Psychological Association, www.apa.org.

This text will enable you to critique both quantitative and qualitative studies. This primer is written in order for students and practitioners to critique either quantitative or qualitative social research studies. Early in the text, you will learn how to distinguish between these and how to select criteria for critiquing each type of study.

The promotion of good research transcends everything else. Above all else, this text seeks to promote good research. Such research is clearly written, logical, purposeful, methodologically sound, knowledge-based, and has implications for various individuals who may benefit from it. By using this primer, students will become better consumers of just what constitutes good research and hopefully will strive for this goal.

Try not to be too cynical or overly confident. My experience has shown that when using critiquing tools such as these, students (or beginning researchers) sometimes get too cynical about the studies they are critiquing. There is a clear line in the sand here between cynicism and skepticism. The primer is written for individuals to be healthy skeptics of social research, not unhealthy cynics of research. Also, individuals should be reminded that just because you may become proficient at critiquing research does not necessarily mean you can conduct or rectify all of the problems you are assessing.

Let's talk about your experiences in critiquing research. I will personally monitor a Web site to dialogue with you about your experiences in using this primer. It will include FAQs (Frequently Asked Questions) and additional readings. This will be available at http://counseling.wadsworth.com/Holoskole.

Layout of the Text

As indicated earlier, every attempt was made to write this primer in a simple, concise, and student-friendly voice. I have come to realize that social research is really not that complicated, so how it is described should also not be complicated. Each section and subsection of the primer specifies minimal criteria as well as a candid commentary about how to critique the various components of the social research study. To do this, criteria are normally listed and explained briefly in a summarizing figure and/or table. These criteria are then condensed into a corresponding box, presented in a checklist fashion for students to check off before proceeding to the next subsection of the research study. Obviously, some sections and subsections of the study will include or achieve all of the criteria listed, while others will not. Thus, students can readily appraise the strengths and weaknesses of any research study, as well as its various components.

In order to assist students in using the figures, tables, and boxes to critique their studies, four graphic prompts are also included. These are GO (to proceed), STOP (to halt), DEFINITION, and PENSIVE PAUSES. The latter are research insights that may require some additional thinking or reading. The intent here is to shepherd the beginning critiquer through any research study, section by section, in an informed and directed manner. I also added some selected quotes by leading male and female thinkers to set the stage for the chapter that follows.

It should also be mentioned that in many cases, the research study you are critiquing may not have the precise headings that are used in this primer. This should not prevent you from using the various subheadings listed here to assess that study. In most cases, the headings presented in the primer represent the most comprehensive itemizing of the various sections and subsections of an "ideal" research study. Often times, authors and/or publishers of social research collapse these sections or subsections for convenience's sake. There are basically three main sections of any quantitative or qualitative research study: Introduction/Purpose, Method, and Results, which encompass the following subsections listed in Figure 1.

Figure 1. Sections and Subsections of a Social Research Study

Three Main Sections	Subsections
	• Title
	• Abstract
	• Author's Affiliation
I. Introduction/Purpose	
	• Review of Literature
	• Rationale for Study
	• Purpose of the Study
II. Method	
	• Sample Selection
	• Study Design
	• Data Collection Procedures
	• Instruments of Study
III. Results	
	• Findings
	• Discussion
	• Limitations
	• Implications

Figure 1 provides the main and subsection headings you can use in critiquing any social research study you are examining.

2

Science or Not?
Research or Not?
Science and Research

Science is the refusal to believe on the basis of hope.
– Carrie P. Snow

And in the beginning...there was science, the basis of all research as we know it today. Science is a complex concept that has been differentially defined and interpreted by scientists and non-scientists alike. Rather than enter this definitional debate, it is easier to simplify what we know about science and relate it to critiquing and understanding research.

First off, we know that science is not intuition, common sense, opinion, or conjecture, although ironically all of these may be used in science. It is linked to research because all research uses a scientific method of some sort, or it cannot be called research. Science is the context, then, for the conduct of all research, as it provides certain laws, principles, or tenets to which all research must adhere. Since the various research studies you will be critiquing (and hopefully eventually conducting one day) are likely to be in your specialized field of study in the social and behavioral sciences (e.g., social work, psychology, nursing, public administration, education, law), let's look at how science is linked to research by using social work as an example (see Figure 2).

Figure 2. The Relationship Between Science, Research, Social Research, and Social Work Research

SCIENCE

RESEARCH

SOCIAL RESEARCH

SOCIAL WORK RESEARCH

Figure 2 uses social work research as the example here, but any field of study in the social and behavioral sciences could be substituted in its place (e.g., sociology, psychology, nursing, education). It is first important to understand that these activities (in Figure 2) are presented in a hierarchy, in that all of the elements of the tier above are included in the one below. Thus, social work research is part of social research is part of research which, by default, is part of science.

As one might assume, some of the laws, principles, or tenets of science hold more applicability to research than others. These are considered, therefore, as minimal scientific tenets that relate to research and are presented in Figure 3.

Figure 3. Minimal Scientific Tenets of All Research Studies

Minimal Tenets	Comments
1. A driving curiosity	Is there a key question, purpose, or need to "get the facts" that is central to the study?
2. Systematic observation	Is there a repeated or reinforced observation of the facts or phenomena? This is called empiricism.
3. Systematic method	Is there systematic testing or experimentation in the study that conforms to established research procedures?
4. Logical inquiry	Does the study follow logical inquiry? The two forms which generally prevail here are deduction (moving from specific to general) or induction (logic evolves from general to specific).
5. Objectivity	Is the study objective? Objectivity in social science research relates to how transparent or checkable it is. That is, can you repeat this study using these methods or check this study's methods?

Some studies you are critiquing will present themselves as having not only these minimal tenets but others (e.g., ethics, using or generating theory, knowledge acquisition, comparative auspices, rigor). However, at this first critiquing level, you need to look at Figure 3 and corresponding summary Box 1 in order to assess whether the study meets these minimal scientific tenets.

BOX 1: Does the Study Meet the Minimal Scientific Requirements?

Does the study have

- ✓ a driving curiosity
- ✓ a systematic observation
- ✓ a systematic method
- ✓ logical inquiry
- ✓ objectivity

Is It Research?

One may make the assumption that articles published in peer-reviewed social and behavioral science journals are all research studies; however, this is not the case. Within the social work profession, for example, a comprehensive analysis of 13 core professional journals (N = 1,849 articles) over a 5-year period revealed that 47% were deemed as research studies and 53% were deemed non-research (Rosen, Proctor & Staudt, 1999). Similarly, in the Family Preservation Journal, an interdisciplinary journal that a number of different professionals subscribed to, the findings indicated 41% were research and 59% were non-research over a 4-year period (Holosko & Holosko, 1999).

Furthermore, some social science professional journals you will read are more oriented to publishing research studies (e.g., Research on Social Work Practice in social work, Nursing Research in nursing, and Psychological Review in psychology). Other journals in these same fields encourage non-research studies more (e.g., Journal of Women and Social Work in social work, Canadian Nurse in nursing, and Psychological Bulletin in psychology). Therefore, it would seem important here at the outset to define just what we mean by research.

Research is the systematic investigation of a phenomenon. It is the process of searching, investigating, and/or discovering facts by using the scientific method. Social research (see Figure 2) is research about social and behavioral phenomena. Many professionals in respective fields conduct both their unique types of discipline specific research, such as social work research (see Holosko & Leslie, 1997, for a more detailed definition of social work research) and social research investigations outside of their disciplines. In order for the study you are critiquing to be considered as research, then, it must include all of the elements listed in Figure 4. It is important to note here that these are non-mutually exclusive elements (in Figure 4), meaning they all must be present to some degree in order for the study to be classified as a research study.

Figure 4. Basic Elements of All Research Studies

Elements	Comments
1. A specified purpose	This may take the form of a research question, study objectives, statement of purpose, or hypothesis.
2. A rationale for study	This is the stated reason(s) for conducting the study, a literature review, or a review of pertinent theories.
3. A specified method	This minimally includes a sample and the study procedure.
4. Analysis of data	This may be in summarized narrative, descriptive, tabular, or graph form.
5. A conclusion	This is typically concluding remarks, a discussion of the study's findings, or implications of the study.

Many published articles you will read in journals may have started out as bona fide research studies, but along the way, either the study itself or subsections of it were written up as non-research studies (e.g., a review of literature, a theoretical framework). These articles often require a careful rereading because the authors may still refer to them as research (their origin), but as published, they cannot be considered as a research study in your critique.

Corresponding Box 2 for Figure 4 allows you to determine whether the article you are critiquing is a research study.

BOX 2: Is It a Research Study?

Does the study have all of the following?

- ✓ a specified purpose
- ✓ a rationale
- ✓ a specified method
- ✓ analysis of data
- ✓ a conclusion

Non-Research Studies

Although this text is about critiquing research studies only, it is important for you to understand what constitutes a non-research study. Also, you should be made aware that although the philosophers of science remind us that ideally good research yields good knowledge, sometimes this doesn't happen. That is, some well-written research studies produce very little in the way of "new knowledge." Conversely, knowledge emanating from philosophic, historical, spiritual, and non-research worlds have contributed immeasurably to our understanding of many important discoveries and complex phenomena, advancing our thinking considerably in the process.

A non-research study may have one, two, three, or four of the elements of research studies listed in Figure 4, but not all of them (remember, they are non-mutually exclusive of one another). As a result, it would be deemed a non-research study. Upon reviewing numerous non-research studies in a number of professional journals, they generally take the forms listed in Figure 5.

Figure 5. Typical Types of Non-Research Studies in Social and Behavioral Research Journals

Types	Comments
1. Literature Reviews	These are overviews of literature, synthesis/analysis of literature, or summaries of literature.
2. Critiques of...	These are critiques of laws, programs, policies, methods, cases, literature, theories, treatment methods, etc. They typically do not follow an ascribed method or procedure and are idiosyncratic to the authors' analytic perspective.
3. Descriptions of Research Methods	These present information about research methodologies, and they do not have a substantive research focus. They basically inform about how and why a research methodology was used and its effectiveness.

Sometimes you may find non-research studies which combine some of the three types listed in Figure 5, for example, a literature review and a critique of social policies. By using

Figures 4 and 5 together, you now have a way of determining a research from a non-research study. So before you check off Box 3, make sure that you simultaneously check Box 2.

BOX 3: Is It a Non-research Study?

Is the study just

✓ a literature review
✓ a critique of something or
✓ a description of a research methodology

This stop sign is a warning to you that if you checked yes to any criteria in Box 3, above, you need to return to the library or journals and find a research study to critique.

3

Qualitative vs. Quantitative Research

To acquire knowledge, one must study, but to acquire wisdom, one must observe.
– Marilyn vos Savant

Congratulations! You now have successfully located a study that is both scientific and, as published, is classified as a research study. You must now determine whether it is a qualitative or quantitative study. You need to understand some features of both of these studies so that you may become a more astute consumer of social research.

First off, it is important for beginning research students not to be pulled into the unnecessary debate and polarization over which method is better, qualitative or quantitative. They are both research, they both are scholarly, they both follow scientific tenets, and both have contributed to knowledge acquisition. However, you should be aware of their similarities and/or differences.

In the past fifty years or so in North America, qualitative research has evolved from the previously deemed "other method" of empirical research to an "alternative method." This represents a considerable shift in how many disciplines and professions have come to accept, use, teach, and embrace qualitative research. Indeed, there have been numerous well-written qualitative research texts in the fields of psychology, sociology, anthropology, social work, nursing, and education, among others.

Qualitative research is the systematic, firsthand observation of real world phenomena. This definition implies that the researcher actively participates in the real world s/he is studying and as such, becomes an active part of the investigation (Filstead, 1970, p. 103). *Quantitative research systematically explores, describes, or tests variables by studying them in numerical or statistical form.*

Table 1 presents some of the selected differences between qualitative (QL) and quantitative (QN) research. It is important to note that there are areas of overlap between quantitative and qualitative research in each of the selected criteria listed in Table 1. For example, both may produce descriptive data (Criteria #1), or both may incorporate aspects of phenomenology and positivism (Criteria #2), etc. So for each criterion listed, these differences hold true for the most part, but not absolutely.

Table 1. Selected Differences Between Qualitative and Quantitative Social Research

Selected Criteria	Qualitative (QL)	Quantitative (QN)
1. Main Purpose	To describe and understand individuals and/or events in natural settings	To explore, describe, test, or assess phenomena
2. Theoretical Perspective	Interpretative	Positivism
3. Logical Orientation	Inductive (G → S)	Hypothetico -deductive (S → G)
4. Dynamicism	Process oriented: experiential and systematic	Deterministic: linear and prescribed
5. Theory Use and Generation	Integrated throughout, requisite grounded theory	To justify hypothesis questions, and to validate
6. Researcher's Role	Active (immersion)	Passive (immersion optional)
7. Problem Specification	May emerge at the end	Early on
8. Method	Create as you evolve	Pre-determined
9. Generalizability	Low	High

Since some of these differences and terms may be unfamiliar to you, they will be briefly elaborated upon here. (For a more comprehensive overview of these issues and their differences in the social and behavioral sciences, see Holosko, 2001.)

Purpose

Qualitative research's express purpose is to produce descriptive data in an individual's own written or spoken words and/or observable behavior. So whether the topic of study is an individual, family, event, behavior, agency, organization, and/or culture, all QL research yields descriptive data foremost. Quantitative (QN) social research, however, may also produce descriptive data, but these are normally in quantitative descriptive (numeric or statistical) form. Its purpose can also be to explore phenomena; test ideas, assumptions, or variables; or assess/ evaluate something (e.g., a practice intervention, a human service program or policy).

Philosophical Perspective

Also referred to as epistemology, QL research is primarily interpretative. QN research is primarily positivistic. The former is defined as being concerned with understanding the meaning of human experience from the subject's own frame of reference. Thus, reality is defined by the research participant's interpretations of his or her own subjective reality (Grinnell, Jr., and Unrau, 2005, p. 76). The latter, referred to as positivism, empirically seeks the facts or causes of social phenomena based on experimentally derived evidence and/or valid observations.

Logical Orientation

QL social research primarily works from an inductive point of view or a general perspective that does not require rigorously defined questions and hypotheses. As such, these studies evolve from the "facts up" and logically proceed from a general point of view to a specific conclusion, set of questions, hypotheses, or grounded theory (Tutty et al., 1996). QN social research, for the most part, works from the problem question or "theory down" to a generalizable conclusion. In this hypothetico-deductive process, data are collected and the assumptions or hypotheses are determined and operationalized; the assumptions or hypotheses are then assessed for their validity.

Dynamism

QL social research by its very nature is process-oriented, whereby the researcher enters the natural setting and touches, feels, lives, and observes the subject(s) of study (e.g., the individual, family, group, agency, and/or community). This experiential perspective is a requisite for collecting rich, contextual, and complete descriptive data. Thus, one observation shapes the perception of the other, and vice versa. QN social research typically follows a more deterministic lock-step process: problem statement → literature review → testable assumptions/hypotheses → data collection → conclusion. Although some QN social research methods allow for the researcher to be more experientially and actively involved in his or her study (e.g., single-system designs), the researcher's role is still largely detached and is oriented toward following the linear steps previously described.

Theory Use and Generation

QL social researchers may or may not use theory to assist them in the subjects of their investigations and some argue that rigorously defined questions or hypotheses emanating from theory delimits such research. Concepts, ideas, and questions which guide their work often emerge during the course of their study in response to what they observe, not to preordained theories or beliefs (Tutty et al., 1996, p.12). Further, it is an implicit requirement of QL research that the conclusions of their studies result in simple explanatory or middle-range theory, referred to as "grounded theory" (Schatzman & Strauss, 1973).

Theory in QN research is first used to derive the testable assumptions/hypotheses of the study. It is then used during the data analyses or end-stage of the study, whereby the data collected are presented to verify or negate the theory from which the testable assumptions/hypotheses were formulated. The push to grounded theory to explain findings is not a requisite of this method, and as a result, many social researchers do not generate any theory per se from their studies.

Researcher's Role

As indicated in the previous definition, all QL research requires the researcher to be actively immersed in the natural environment s/he is observing. The subjective lens that the researcher brings to the subject of the study is an important part of such research. QN research does not require this, and for the most part, the researcher has a passive and detached role. Some social research, however, such as practice or program evaluation, requires a researcher to become more involved in the settings in which their investigations take place. But even in such cases, the researcher generally assumes a value-neutral and objective role during the course of the study.

Problem Specification

QL research often avoids specifying the problem of study early on. Indeed, the actual phenomena being studied may not be apparent until the very end of the investigation. Conversely, QN research requires clear problem specification and operationalization of study variables from the onset.

Method

This term generally encompasses the study design, sample, study procedure, and data collection. QL social research allows the method to unfold during the course of the investigation. The researcher then flexibly crafts the method to suit the evolving study requirements. So concerns such as how many observations should be made, how many interviews should take place, which questions should one ask respondents, etc., are all usually unknown until the researcher gets to that step in the investigation. QN social research, however, usually predetermines the method by planning it carefully, ideally pre-testing aspects of it (e.g., its feasibility, length of time for data collection, and instrumentation) and describing it in detail.

Generalizability

Generalizability is attributed to two components of research: the method and findings. In QL social research, because their methods often use unique or purposive samples, abnormal events, and/or anomalies, findings are not targeted to precise but more general conclusions. As such, their generalizability is deemed low. QN research, however, strives for more precise measurement and findings. For instance, standardized instruments are encouraged, random samples are often selected which can generalize to populations, and parametric statistics are often selected which can generalize to populations. Their findings are normally answers to the questions posed at the beginning of the study and are stated in precise and qualified ways to enhance their overall generalizability.

Overall, Table 1 outlined a number of selected differences between QL social research and QN social research. Many disciplines such as social work, sociology, and nursing (among others) have been highly successful in utilizing both QL and QN research and lately have encouraged the use of both methods concurrently (Cowger & Menon, 2001).

STOP! Now go back to the study you are critiquing and assess whether it is qualitative or quantitative. If it is qualitative...

GO! You may proceed to Chapter 9 in the text and critique it according to the criteria listed there. You may also use the criteria in Chapters 4 through 8 as needed, because many apply to both (see Appendix A for a cross-listing of these respective criteria).

If it satisfies the criteria for a quantitative study only...

GO! Proceed to the next chapter.

4

Writing Clarity, Title, Author's Affiliation, Abstract, and References

If one cannot state a matter clearly enough so that even a 12-year-old can understand it, one should remain within the cloistered walls of the university and laboratory until one gets a better grasp of one's subject matter.
– Margaret Mead

Before you start critiquing in greater depth the main components of the research study you have located, some other issues need to be critiqued. These are writing clarity, title, abstract, author's affiliation, and references.

Writing Clarity

Approximately 85% of the published professional research journals used in the social and behavioral science fields require authors to use the American Psychological Associations' (APA) publication guidelines.

I encourage all students to purchase the manual, as it not only sets the standard for stylistic requirements, but is written clearly and demonstrates how the content of a research paper can be constructively directed by its writing using the APA format. Outside of its specification of writing requirements, the manual has been used to spin-off numerous student friendly texts such as Mastering APA Style: Student's Workbook and Framing Guide, H. Gelfund and C. Walker (1995); Dissertations from Start to Finish, J. Cone and S. Foster (1995); Writing with Style: APA Style for Social Work (2004), L. Szuchman and B. Thomlinson; and the APA-Style Helper (2000), www.apa.org/apa-style, which is software you can download to write research term papers, reports, review articles, etc.

We need not go over the numerous APA stylistic requirements published in the manual but rather shall distill some core elements related to research writing, which can be used to critique this aspect of the study. These are presented in Figure 6.

Figure 6. Elements Related to Clarity of Research Writing

Writing Elements	Comments
1. Are there three core subsections evident in the article?	Can you identify minimally an introduction, method, and results?
2. Clarity of ideas, findings, and discussion	Is the tone of the article clear in expressing the author's ideas, findings, and discussion?
3. The central point is evident.	As you read the article carefully, is the central point of the article evident and clearly expressed?
4. 5-cent vs. 10-cent words	When you read the study does it have fancy 10-cent words or simpler 5-cent words? Good writers try not to use a 10-cent word when they can use a 5-cent word instead.
5. Phraseology, wordiness, redundancy and jargon	Phraseology and wordiness refers to the author's over-reliance on phrases or words that are unclear or unnecessary (e.g., based on the fact that = because; distinctively different = choose one or the other of these words). Ask yourself, if three pages were eliminated from this study, would it matter? Redundancy means saying the same thing over and over again, in similar or different ways. It is a writing curse that many researchers have, so watch for it. Another writing curse is the overuse of technical terminology and jargon.
6. Three readings and you're out!	Carefully reread the study three times. If after three readings you still don't know what it is about, STOP! Go and get another article to critique which is more clearly written.

The APA manual, as well as other stylistic texts, specifies the issues of writing more comprehensively than what is being presented here. You should refer to them accordingly. Research writing is not the same as narrative or essay writing, and it is a skill that all researchers work on. One is also reminded that the use of APA stylistic requirements does not necessarily mean that the study is clearly written. In critiquing the writing clarity then, examine Box 4 and assess these summarized requirements.

BOX 4: Is the Study Clearly Written?

When you reread the study

- ✓ can you discern the three core subsections?
- ✓ are the ideas clearly presented?
- ✓ is the central point evident?
- ✓ does it use more 5-cent than 10-cent words?
- ✓ does it avoid cumbersome phrases, wordiness, and redundancy?
- ✓ is it understandable after three readings?

Title

You will come across a variety of titles for research reports. Many students have expressed some dismay over the fact that sometimes the title of a study initially captured their interest, but after reading the study, the content really didn't materialize in the way in which the title had promised.

Titles of research studies need to be accurate, properly written, and should avoid rhetorical questions. In regard to the latter, a title such as "Depressed Women: What About Them?" leaves too much interpretation, speculation, and in this case, characterization. The title is not only important, but it should be succinct, accurate, and convey precisely what the study is about. Figure 7 provides a list of features for writing a proper research title.

Figure 7. Features of an Appropriate Research Title

Features	Comments
1. It should have 10-12 words.	This is the recommended length by APA.
2. It should make sense standing alone.	It should be logical, clear, and make sense as you read it, independent of the research study.
3. It should name the important study variables or theoretical issues.	These should be cited clearly in the title.
4. Makes reference to the sample.	The title should have a reference to the sample that it studied.
5. Identifies relationships among variables.	It should identify relationships between the main study variables.
6. Avoids being cutesy, posing rhetorical questions, and using jargon.	Cutesy titles have no place in research writing. Good titles also avoid posing rhetorical questions and using jargon.

Now check the title of the research report you have obtained and read the corresponding summary in Box 5.

BOX 5: Assessing the Title

Does the title

- ✓ have 10 to 12 words?
- ✓ make sense standing alone?
- ✓ name important variables/ theoretical issues?
- ✓ make reference to the study sample?
- ✓ identify variable relationships?
- ✓ avoid cutesiness, rhetorical questions, and jargon?

Author's Affiliation

All authors who produce and submit research studies are required to indicate their credentials and employment affiliations. Although most professional academic journals include these in their published accounts, a few do not. If the study you are critiquing publishes them, you can learn a lot from these affiliations.

You should first be made aware that the vast majority of authors who publish research in professional journals are academics. Although this has created a schism between researchers and practitioners in some professional fields like social work (see Holosko & Leslie, 1997), most academics in higher education are actively engaged in research to enhance knowledge in their respective professional fields.

By examining the affiliation of the authors, you can determine where the authors work, their degree status, and their relationship to where the research was conducted. This may give you further insight about the study you are critiquing. If, for example, an author held the position of evaluator at a health or human service agency and published a study using data from this agency, such a study is likely to be a favorable evaluation of an intervention or program at that agency. In addition, with the advance of the warp-speed World Wide Web, you can usually quickly locate where the author works and if they have conducted other studies in this area to give you additional insight.

You should also note that there is a hierarchal pecking order in the listings of multiple authors. In most professional or academic fields, normally the first author is the main author and principal researcher (and s/he probably did most of the work). In medicine, however, the main author or principal investigator is normally the final person listed. Use Box 6 to help you to assess the authors' affiliations more appropriately.

BOX 6: What Are the Authors' Affiliations?

Can you find out

- ✓ where the authors work?
- ✓ their degree status?
- ✓ their relationship to the study?
- ✓ any additional information about them?

Abstract

The abstract is a brief summary of the contents of the research study. Like the title, it is used for abstracting, indexing, or for computerized search engines to retrieve articles. It has been said that the single most important paragraph you will read in any study is the abstract. Figure 8 lists attributes of well-written abstracts.

Figure 8. Elements of Well-Written Abstracts

Elements	Comments
1. Conciseness	APA recommends not exceeding 120 words or 960 characters and spaces.
2. Clarity	Define all abbreviations (except units of measurement), acronyms, and unique terms.
3. Accuracy	Make sure that it reports accurate information which is in the body of the accompanying study.
4. Specificity	It needs a good lead sentence to catch the reader's eye. It also minimally requires the purpose, method, 2 to 3 of the major study findings, and implications.
5. Active Voice	It is written in the present (not past) tense.

Box 7 summarizes the points from Figure 8 and helps you to critique a well-written abstract.

BOX 7: Assessing the Abstract

Is the abstract

✓ concise, clear, and accurate?
✓ specific?
✓ written in the active voice?

References

One of the benefits of research studies is that they typically have extensive reference citations. Many students who critique research studies often track other studies of interest from the reference list at the back of the study or article. For the record, the citations at the end of a research study are called references, not bibliographies, as they are sometimes referred to.

A convenient way to critique references is by applying the recency and relevancy "15-10" rule of thumb. This means that the research study should have a minimum of 15 cited references (if possible), and they should be current, meaning most of those published in the last decade. This is a general critiquing guideline, and there will be some exceptions to this, of course. Box 8 offers a quick and simple way to critique the references in the study you are assessing.

BOX 8: Assessing the References: The "15-10" Rule of Thumb

Are there

✓ at least 15 different references cited?

In addition,

✓ are a majority of these recent--occurring in the past 10 years?

5

The Three Main Content Areas of the Quantitative Research Article: Introduction, Method, and Results

The whole of science is nothing more than a refinement of everyday thinking.
– A. Einstein

There are basically three main content areas of any quantitative research study: Introduction, Method and Results. Different journals, research reports, and authors may use different titles for these, but they represent the main cornerstone subsections of any well-written quantitative study. Each has minimal subheadings (specified or not) that need addressing as follows:

1. Introduction - Review of Literature and Purpose
2. Method - Sample, Procedures, Measures
3. Results - Discussion, Implications

Later on, ways of critiquing each of these, as well as their respective subsections, will be elaborated on and presented.

At this first level of appraising a quantitative research study or article, you must determine whether the three main subsections are clearly delineated and related one to another. In regard to the latter, Figure 9 depicts an arrow logically connecting these sections, as well as some basic questions to consider when appraising them both individually and as a set.

Figure 9. The Relationship Between the Introduction, Method and Results

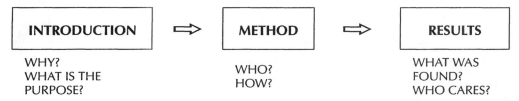

INTRODUCTION	⇨	METHOD	⇨	RESULTS
WHY? WHAT IS THE PURPOSE?		WHO? HOW?		WHAT WAS FOUND? WHO CARES?

To elaborate (on Figure 9), if a research study is well-written, these three sections will follow each other logically. For example, the introduction clearly relates to the purpose, which in turn, relates to the method and then the results. This logical research progression is called "centrality of purpose."

At this first level of critiquing the study, another way to appraise these subsections is to ask yourself upon reading each section the underpinning questions as indicated in Figure 9, now elaborated upon in Box 9.

BOX 9: Initially Appraising the Introduction, Method, and Results of the Research Study

After reading each subsection of the research study, answer the following questions:

I. Introduction

• Why is this study being done?
• What is the purpose of this study?

II. Method

• With whom is this study being done?
• How is the study being done?

III. Results

• What was found in this study?
• Who can benefit from these findings?

Box 9 represents a simple way to begin your critique of the research study. In the following chapters, these questions and others will be presented in greater depth. Whether you realize it or not, your critical-thinking antennae are now on as you scrutinize the study before you. If you feel comfortable wearing these antennae...

Go! Proceed to the next chapter.

6

Introduction: Review of the Literature and Study Purpose

I was brought up to believe that the only thing worth doing was to add the sum of accurate information in the world.
– Margaret Mead

Introduction

The actual title "Introduction" is seldom used in the study itself; nonetheless, the first section of the study is called the Introduction. As indicated earlier in Chapter 5, the Introduction has two subsections (which may or may not be specified) embedded within it, the Review of Literature and Purpose of the Study. Normally, the literature review precedes the purpose. Sometimes, however, the purpose is stated before the literature or is embedded within it. As a whole, the Introduction section should answer the simple question, "Why is this study being conducted and what is its purpose?" (See Figure 9 and Box 9.) If upon rereading the Introduction you cannot assess why this study is being done or what the purpose is, you should note this as a major shortcoming of the study. You should not have to read the entire study in order to understand the answers to these key questions.

Review of the Literature

Earlier (in Chapter 4), I mentioned a quick and simple way to assess the references of the study by using the R&R (recency and relevance rule) or the "15-10" rule of thumb. This is the section in which the majority of literature reviewed by the authors is presented. The literature presented here basically serves as corroborating evidence for the study. As such, it provides the context or backdrop for the entire study.

The actual heading "Literature Review" is used infrequently. However, the authors assemble the literature that they reviewed for the study, usually organizing their review from general or related literature to more specific literature. This means that as you read on in the Introduction, the studies cited are likely to be more closely and specifically related to the purpose of the study. In addition, if the literature review is extensive, it may be organized by using one or two subheadings.

Well-written and comprehensive literature reviews are sometimes more insightful and interesting to students than the actual study which follows. This is particularly true if the study was methodologically remiss and/or did not provide any meaningful findings or implications. In this regard, many students who are either critiquing or conducting research scour studies for well-written and comprehensive literature reviews.

Figure 10 provides five criteria which can be used to critique the literature review portion of the Introduction.

Figure 10. Critiquing the Literature Review

Elements	Comments
1. What is the P.O.I. of the phenomena being studied?	Can you determine the Prevalence (P), Occurrence (O), and Incidence (I) of the phenomena which is being studied?
2. Is this a balanced (pro and con) literature review?	Do the authors present both pro and con literature to back up their study? Although there is a natural tendency to include only pro (or supportive) literature in this section, good reviews also reflect some balance and con (or non-supportive) studies.
3. The rationale is clear.	After reading the literature review, are the reasons for doing this study clear?
4. The literature justifies the approach.	Is the literature presented first related to the topic of study? Second, does it clearly justify the purpose of the study?
5. Adequacy	Is the review of the literature adequate? You may wish to revisit the "15-10" rule of thumb here in order to assess its adequacy and comprehensiveness.

By using Figure 10, you can now critique the literature presented in the Introduction of the study, as summarized in Box 10.

BOX 10: Assessing the Literature Review in the Introduction

Is the Literature Review presented in the Introduction

✓   presented so that you can determine the P.O.I. of the study?
✓   a balanced review?
✓   clearly apparent in its rationale?
✓   presented in a manner which justifies the purpose of the study?
✓   adequate?

Study Purpose

Normally at the end of the Literature Review, the authors state the study purpose. If the study purpose is not apparent in the Introduction, the study should not have passed peer review and/ or should not have been published. This is indeed a serious faux pas, as how can one present a study if s/he doesn't know what it is about? Clearly stated and easily identified study purposes are the preferred norm for any responsible social researcher.

As indicated in Figure 11, the purpose can be stated in one or more of four ways.

Figure 11. Types of Study Purposes Typically Used by Social Researchers

Types	Comments
1. Explicitly Stated Statement of Purpose	This includes a sentence usually beginning with the phrase "The purpose of this study is to..."
2. Objectives	These are an actual listing of study objectives, which are purposes of the study. They can be serialized (e.g., 1, 2, 3) and/or listed as primary (or major) or secondary (or minor) objectives.
3. Research Questions	These are a series of questions that the study is hoping to answer.
4. Hypotheses	Hypotheses are stated in one of two forms. One is directional, meaning the authors connect the variables in an applied way (e.g., those people who wear large hats are also likely to wear large shoes). The other form is the null hypothesis, in which there is no relationship implied between the variables being studied--but the authors really hope that there is (e.g., there is no relationship between hat size and shoe size among people). Hypotheses are either serialized in list form (1, 2, 3, etc.) or listed as major or minor.

Latent Purposes

Often upon reading the entire research study, another purpose unfolds; for example, the instruments/scales used in the study were tested as reliable and valid, and can be used with similar populations. This is referred to as a latent purpose, or one that emerged as a result of the conduct of the study. Although this was not a central purpose stated earlier in the Introduction, students should be mindful of emerging latent purposes when critiquing the overall purpose of the study.

Implied Purpose or the Purpose Behind the Purpose

Sometimes there is an implied purpose, or a purpose behind the stated purpose of the study. Examples of such purposes include (1) showing that an intervention worked so a program may receive more money, prestige, credibility, etc., (2) negating the phenomena being studied to provide a different perspective to what we have come to know about it (for any number of reasons), (3) helping a social science academic receive promotion or tenure, and (4) making a case for a stakeholder with a vested interest in a phenomena (e.g., a larger political/government agenda behind the research). Although discerning these are difficult for the beginning research consumer, s/he should be aware of their presence and acknowledge them whenever possible.

7

Method: Sample Selection, Study Design, Data Collection Procedures, and Materials

When testing the depth of a stream, do not use both feet.
– Chinese Proverb

The Overall Method

The Method section of any research study represents its heart and soul. Above all else, it basically answers the core questions what happened to whom, how, and why. Researchers place great emphasis on detailing their methods, and for good reason. First, others may wish to replicate the study to enhance its generalizability. Second, attention to methodological detail demonstrates the authors' thinking, assumptions, scientific rigor, and the realities and obstacles to conducting the actual study. Third, others may wish to use particular aspects of the Method in their own studies (e.g., a sampling technique, a procedure, a scale or instrument, interview schedule).

The Method normally includes four main areas: Sample Selection, Study Design, Data Collection Procedures, and Materials. Authors typically use two of these methodological subheadings or versions of them in their published research reports. Each of these, then, will be scrutinized, and criteria for critiquing them will be outlined.

Sample Selection

In this subsection, sometimes called Participants, Subjects, The Sample, Sampling, or The Sample and Population, the authors specify how the sample was selected. Minimally included in such specification are the size of the sample, techniques used in selecting it, its relationship to the population, the time it took to obtain the sample, and any unique features of it. These are elaborated upon and presented as critiquing criteria in Figure 12.

Figure 12. Critiquing the Sample Selection

Elements of the Sample	Comments
1. Size	Statisticians define a large sample as n > 250, and a small sample as n < 30.
2. Techniques Used in Selection	First, is there a technique mentioned (e.g., how did the authors obtain the sample for this study)? Second, do they label the technique procedurally (e.g., random sampling, random assignment to condition, cluster sampling, snowball sampling, convenience sampling, quota sampling)?
3. Relationship to the Population	Do the authors specify the sample's (n's) relationship to the population (N)? Example: its size vis-a-vis the N's size, its N generalizability, its biasness, etc.
4. Time Frame for Selection	How long did it take to obtain the sample?
5. Other Unique Features	Does the sample present any unique features (e.g., its cultural context, its relationship to treatment samples, difficulties in obtaining it, specific characteristics)?

As indicated in Figure 12, in order to critique the sample, one has to check off the criteria list in Box 11.

BOX 11: Assessing the Sample Selection

Critique the sample selection with respect to

✓   its size
✓   techniques used in selection
✓   its relationship to the population
✓   its time frame
✓   other unique features

Study Design

At this point, the authors must articulate how the study was designed. Many authors use accepted designs (e.g., descriptive, quantitative-descriptive, experimental, or quasi-experimental). It is helpful when critiquing study designs that you eventually learn how to schematically draw or map out the design in an effort to critique it more clearly. These symbols will be explained in more detail in the forthcoming design parameters subsection. For the most part, these symbols are idiosyncratic to different professions.

Figure 13 describes the set of criteria which may be used to critique the first set, study design elements.

Figure 13. Critiquing the First Set of Study Design Elements

Design Elements	Comments
1. Time	How long did it take to complete this study?
2. Groups	How many groups or subgroups were used in the study design?
3. Replicability	Can this design be replicated?
4. Internal or External Threats	Are there any internal or external threats in this study as designed? These may include issues such as history, maturation, selection, testing, experimenter expectancy, generalizability, etc.

Corresponding Box 12 provides a summary of these criteria.

BOX 12: Critiquing the First Set of Study Design Elements

Examine the study design with respect to

✓ time
✓ groups used
✓ replicability
✓ internal or external threats

Major Classification Type

All empirical studies seek the acquisition of knowledge as their overarching purpose. Quantitative studies can conceptually be classified as one of four main types: descriptive, quantitative-descriptive, experimental, or quasi-experimental. For those familiar with the history of such classification types (see, for example, Tripodi, Fellin, & Meyer,1983, or Grinnell Jr., 1995), you will note that social scientists have moved beyond the debate of including exploratory as one of these main types. The short story here is really rather simple--all empirical research by its very nature is exploratory. Indeed, exploration is tied to the very definition of research (see Chapter 2). As a result, it is a dated and redundant design typology as it underpins all of these other classification types. Later on, you will see how this exploratory notion is retained in quantitative studies.

In order to classify the study as such, the reader needs to pull back a bit from the Method section and examine in retrospect the overall purpose of the study. This requires one to read and probably reread the entire study, carefully appraising its central purpose and methods used together in the investigation.

Table 2 can be used to complete this task, as it provides definitions for these four major types of quantitative social research.

Table 2. Four Major Classification Types of Quantitative Social Research

Type	Purpose
1. Descriptive	To describe a phenomenon for some purpose (e.g., to delineate features of it, to develop hypotheses or questions, to modify our thinking of it, or to add to our knowledge of the phenomenon).
2. Quantitative-Descriptive	To describe and quantify variables and relate them to each other. For example, what variables impact on others and why?
3. Experimental	Their explicit purpose is to test the relationship between independent (treatment) and dependent (outcome) variables. In order to be classified as a true experimental study, all of the following criteria must be present: (1) randomization, (2) a manipulated treatment condition (X), (3) a comparison or control group who does not receive any treatment condition, and (4) specification of hypotheses.
4. Quasi-Experimental	Having the same purpose as experimental, quasi-experimental studies require some, but not all, of the criteria in 3 (above) to be present; thus they "approximate" experimental studies.

Box 13, then, provides a checklist for determining the type of quantitative research study you are critiquing. Remember that some studies may overlap these types (e.g., descriptive and quantitative-descriptive), but upon developing critical appraisal skills, one of these overriding classification types is prominent and can be determined.

BOX 13: Determining the Study Type

Is the research

✓ Descriptive
✓ Quantitative-Descriptive
✓ Experimental
✓ Quasi-Experimental

Design Objectives

After determining which of the major designs your study follows, you should then assess its design objective. That is, what is the overall design of this study actually trying to achieve? Figure 14 outlines the four main objectives of quantitative research studies.

Figure 14: Design Objectives of Quantitative Research Studies

Objectives	Comments
1. Exploration	To explore in-depth a phenomenon, event, population, intervention, interaction, culture, etc., in order to acquire more knowledge about it.
2. Instrument/Development Scale	To develop an instrument, scale, inventory, interview schedule, assessment tool, or way of measuring a phenomenon and test its utility for use by others.
3. Variable Relationships	To test the relationships between variables for determining how they impact, associate, predict, or influence each other.
4. Evaluation Research	To assess the impact of a specific program or intervention on individuals by determining its activities and outcomes. These can be evaluations of practice or evaluations of programs.

Corresponding Box 14 summarizes these main design objectives of quantitative studies.

BOX 14: Assessing the Design Objectives

What is the main objective of this study design?

- ✓ Exploratory
- ✓ Instrument/Scale Development
- ✓ Variable Relationship
- ✓ Evaluation of Practice and/or Programs

Design Parameters

Each study is designed in a way so that the researchers may optimally collect data about the phenomena being studied. How they collect their data is usually determined by resources, time, convenience, opportunity or fate, and/or how they mapped out or planned their study design. The study plan is the researcher's "road map," which helps to systematize all data collection. This ensures both the consistency of data collection and scientific integrity of the study. In turn, this enhances the generalizability of the Method part of the overall study.

Before describing the design parameters, it is important to acquaint yourself with some of the basic symbols or nomenclature used in mapping out the study plan or schema. D. Campbell and J. Stanley formally introduced these to social science researchers in 1963 in their watershed text *Experimental and Quasi-Experimental Designs for Research*.

Table 3 describes some of the more familiar symbols used in mapping out the design parameters.

Table 3. Typical Symbols Used in Mapping the Design Parameters

Main Symbols Used	Description/Comments
1. O	The "Observation" of a phenomenon. In social research this observation is usually by use of a questionnaire, survey, interview, observation schedule, shared experience, or a secondary data source (e.g. assessment forms, census). The O is really how and where the researcher collected the data and/or observed the phenomena. A subscripted O (O_1, O_2, O_3, etc.) means these were multiple observations of the phenomena and therefore, multiple data collection points.
2. X	Capital letter X is the main treatment effect or intervention given to the sample in the study. This is almost always a planned or contrived intervention that should be defined in precise research ways. This means it should minimally have a time frame in which it was given, goals and objectives, activities, and expected outcomes. Like O, it may be offered once or repeatedly (e.g., X_1, X_2, X_3).
3. R	Capital letter R is the symbol for "Randomness." It is typically used in two ways. One is "Random" selection of a sample, meaning some form of random selection procedure was used in obtaining the sample. It may also mean "Randomization," in that the sample was randomly assigned to a certain treatment condition or particular group (e.g., a comparison/control group, for study purposes).
4. - - - -	These broken lines indicate that there is more than one group in the study (see Box 12). For instance, in Campbell and Stanley's Static-Group Comparison Design (1963), one group received an intervention, while the other did not. This is schematically represented as X O - - - - -- -- O

Now that you have an understanding of some of these basic symbols, you should try to map out the design parameters. Figure 15 identifies the four basic and main design parameters used in social research studies.

Figure 15. The Four Main Design Parameters

Design Parameters	Comments
1. One Shot Case Study With No Intervention O_1	This is when a researcher collects data at one single (and only) entry point, and there is no true intervention or treatment offered. An example would be answering a telemarketing survey over the phone, responding to a survey/interview on the street or in a classroom/hospital, or observing (and recording) who dominates meetings at work.
2. One Shot Case Study With an Intervention XO_1	Here a defined treatment effect or intervention was given to the sample. Data were then collected about its impact (or technically its non-impact). The O_1 normally occurs after the X was administered. For example, students at a university take a statistics course (X); then they receive a final examination testing their knowledge (O_1). Sometimes, the O_1 occurs simultaneous to the X. For instance, a nurse may be studying how patients respond to getting their flu shot from the time they enter the clinic until the time they leave the clinic. Here, the X and O_1 overlap in the study condition.
3. Pre- and Post- Test With an Intervention O_1 X O_2	Here data are collected before the main treatment is given (O_1). This is called the "pre-test"; sometimes, it is called "the baseline." The X occurs for however long it takes to be administered (i.e., for minutes, days, weeks, months, years). Then a post-test (O_2) occurs. For most studies, O_1 and O_2 use the same data collection techniques (e.g., a battery of standardized tests, survey, observation schedule) with the same sample. For example, before a daylong stress management seminar, researchers ask respondents to fill out a survey that assesses their stress-coping skills. After the seminar, they fill out the same survey to determine if the seminar helped them by comparing pre- and post-test scores. You should note that there is a publication bias among social science journals toward those studies which show the treatment (X) worked, to some extent.
4. Multiple Time Series Design With an Intervention O_1 X O_2 O_3 O_4	In this design, pre- and post-tests occur before and after the main treatment (X). Some time elapses and a follow-up study is administered to the sample (O_3). More time elapses and another follow-up study is administered to the same sample (O_4). Here the researchers are trying to determine the long-term impact of the treatment effect. For example, a sample of teenagers is mandated to take a driver's education course focusing on alcohol and drugs. They receive an alcohol and drug awareness inventory (O_1), a driver's education seminar once a week for 12 weeks (X), and then the same alcohol and drug awareness inventory (O_2). At six months (O_3) and 12 months (O_4), they are re-administered the same inventory.

Figure 15 refers only to the basic or four main design parameters that delineate how study data were collected. It is important to note that any of these main design parameters can be modified by (1) adding additional observations (O's) or treatment effects (X's) and/or (2) adding additional groups to the study. In clearly mapping out your study's parameters, you will find it much easier to critique its overall method.

How Many Groups Are There?

As indicated in Figures 13 and 15, the issue of how many groups of subjects needs to be addressed and critiqued. There are basically four main types of groups. These are described in Figure 16.

Figure 16. Main Types of Research Groups

Research Group Types	Comments
1. Case Studies	These are in-depth studies of single or multiple individuals, families, groups, communities, organizations, cultures, phenomena, events, policies, etc. What distinguishes these is their level of analyses, in an effort to find out particular aspects unique to the study purpose.
2. Single Group	This is a singular group of persons who are observed/studied in an effort to collect information about their thinking, feelings, attitudes, knowledge, perceptions, functioning, coping, attributes, etc. What distinguishes these studies from case studies is their purpose--to find out information about the phenomena of interest (e.g., anger, depression, attitudes towards others, communication skills) as it relates to this particular group.
3. Single System Research (SSR)	SSRs focus on a single group (N=1) which may range from an individual or case to a community. They involve the continued observation of one individual/client/system before, during, and after some form of intervention (Bloom, Fischer, Orme, 1999). They are used frequently in the helping professions (e.g., nursing, psychology, family studies, social work, education).
4. Multiple Group	These studies include more than one group of persons in their data collection. A study of a group who received some form of treatment (X) and a comparison group who were not treated would be a multiple group study of two groups.

By using Figure 16 and corresponding Box 15, determine how many groups and which type of group you have in your study.

BOX 15: Type of Research Group

Which type of research group is in your study?

    ✓   Case Studies
    ✓   Single Group
    ✓   Single System Research
    ✓   Multiple Group

Please note that your study may include more than one type of group outlined in Box 15.

Data Collection Procedures

This subsection, also referred to as Procedures, instructs the reader about what was done and also how it was done. Prior to considering these requirements, it is important to first indicate where the study took place (e.g., a school, an emergency room, a classroom). Also, readers should appraise whether primary data collected firsthand or secondary data collected for another purpose (e.g., case records, report cards, hospital records, census tracts) were used for this study, or both. These data collection criteria, as well as others, are presented in Figure 17.

Figure 17. Data Collection Procedures

Criteria	Comments
1. Locale	Where were the data collected?
2. What was done?	What occurred during the collection of data?
3. How were data collected?	How were the data collected?
4. Primary vs. Secondary	Were these primary or secondary data, or both?
5. Time	How long did it take the researchers to collect these data, first by individual case, and then by entire sample?
6. Replicability	Could one readily replicate these data collection procedures?
7. Ethical Considerations	Was there an indication of one or more of the six minimal areas of research ethics: informed consent, voluntarism, right of refusal (without prejudice), respectful of dignity and privacy, risk to benefits, and specification of the purpose of the study?
8. Data Collectors' Relationship to Study Subjects	Specify the relationship between the individuals who collected these data and the actual study subjects.

Corresponding Box 16, then, summarizes these criteria listed in Figure 17 to critiquing the data collection procedures.

> BOX 16: Assessing Data Collection Procedures
>
> Assess the data collection with respect to
>
> ✓ locale
> ✓ what was done
> ✓ how data were collected
> ✓ primary vs. secondary data
> ✓ time
> ✓ replicability
> ✓ ethical considerations
> ✓ relationship to study subjects

Instruments of Study

This area of the Method receives much critical scrutiny because, quite simply, how you measure or assess something determines what you will find out about the phenomena you are studying. Also referred to as Materials, Measures, or both, in this subsection researchers specify how information was transformed from their sample to actual empirical data. A variety of techniques is used by social researchers to obtain data ranging from casual observations of people and events (i.e., recorded in some way) to rigorously controlled clinical testing with repeated and/or multiple measures. The bottom line, though, is that somehow a phenomenon was observed, described, recorded, and/or tested, and then data were generated for research purposes.

Regardless of the materials, measures, and/or instruments used for data collection purposes in social science research, standardized forms are preferred over non-standardized forms. Standardized measures/instruments are those that have been tested for reliability and validity. Non-standardized measures/instruments have not been scrutinized for reliability and/or validity. Typically, social researchers use multiple measures or one instrument, like an inventory that has a number of measures/subscales/inventories within it (i.e., the MMPI).

Figure 18 specifies five criteria used to critique the materials, measures, and/or instruments of study.

Figure 18. Critiquing the Materials Used and Instruments of Study

Elements	Comments
1. Instruments/Scales/ Inventories/Observation Schedules/Questions	What instruments/scales/ inventories/observation schedules/ questions, etc., were used to collect the study data?
2. Materials Used	In addition to the actual instruments of study (e.g., interview schedules, standardized tests, clinical tests), were any other materials used during data collection (e.g., audio/video tapes, reports, manuals, correspondence, computer data)?

Figure 18. continued

Elements	Comments
3. Reliability & Validity	Comment on the researchers' appraisal of the reliability and validity of the various instruments in this study.
4. Replicability	Comment on the ability to replicate the use of all materials and instruments used in this study.
5. Pre-testing	Do the researchers comment on whether these instruments were pre-tested or not?

Box 17 indicates the elements to be considered when critiquing the materials and instruments used in a social science study.

BOX 17: Critiquing the Materials/ Instruments Used

Assess the instruments of the study with respect to

- ✓ instruments/scales/inventories/observation/schedules/questions
- ✓ materials used
- ✓ reliability and validity
- ✓ replicability
- ✓ pre-testing

8

The Results:
The Findings, Discussion,
and Implications

> The problems that exist in the world today cannot be solved by the level of thinking that
> created them.
> – A. Einstein

The final main subsection of the research study is called the Results, and it typically includes the Findings, Discussion, and Implications. These three areas are often clumped under the heading of Results. For critiquing purposes, however, they need to be treated separately. This final major section represents the culmination of the research study where the authors present what they found and what it means. These are the key questions that require answering when critiquing this subsection: What are the main findings of this study? How are they discussed? Who is this study targeted to?

Findings

The findings of the study are typically summarized in tabular, graph, or chart form. Normally, data are presented first, then discussed. One should be reminded that the research study you are critiquing might have been larger and found many other things during the course of its investigation. However, in the article you are critiquing, the authors are only presenting findings they feel are important and/or ones that suit the particular forum (e.g., a journal) in which they are presenting their study. As such, astute students conducting literature searches of academic research journals will recognize how the same study (or versions/parts of it) have been published in different forms across different journals for different intended audiences. This "double dipping," as researchers call it, is not unusual.

Tables/Graphs/Charts

As indicated above, the easiest way to summarize or condense data is by placing them into tables, graphs, and/or charts. Data about the findings may also be presented in narrative form (written in the text), but the use of tables/graphs/charts are preferred due to their simplicity and visual appeal. A general guideline is that six or fewer data points can be presented in the text, but more than that may better lend itself to being portrayed in a table, graph, or chart. Some researchers suffer from "table-itis," in that they either construct too many tables/graphs/charts or present them in confusing ways. Figure 19, followed by corresponding Box 18, outlines criteria for you to use in critiquing the various tables, graphs, and/or charts in your study.

Figure 19. Critiquing the Study's Tables, Graphs, or Charts

Criteria	Comments
1. Number of Tables, Graphs, or Charts	Three or less of any combination of tables, graphs, or charts is the general rule of thumb.
2. Titles	Are the titles of the tables, graphs or charts "stand alone"--meaning you can understand the accompanying table, graph, or chart just by reading the title?
3. Sample Sizes Noted	Are all sample sizes noted in both the title and also within the main column and row headings of the table, graph, or chart?
4. Actual Length	One-half to three-quarter of a page is the preferred length for any table, graph, or chart.
5. Clarity	Are data presented in the table, graph, or chart clearly understood?

Corresponding Box 18 provides the summary checklist of these criteria as indicated in Figure 19.

BOX 18: Critiquing Tables, Graphs, or Charts

Assess the study's tables, graphs, or charts:

    ✓   number used
    ✓   their titles
    ✓   whether sample sizes are noted
    ✓   their length
    ✓   clarity of data presentation

Statistics

The first thing researchers should do when they present their data is to describe what they found. The second thing they typically do is to test for things statistically in their data set (e.g., by comparing variables, comparing one group to another such as treatment vs. control, determining the relationship between the treatment variable (X) and certain outcomes). In order to first describe their data, social researchers use descriptive statistics.

These are simply numerical descriptors of the data. They typically include frequencies, percentages, the mean or arithmetic average ($\overline{X}$), the mode or the most frequently occurring number (Mo), the median or that number in which 50% of the number set is above and 50% fall below (Me), and the standard deviation or how far things vary from the mean in a standard way (SD). Descriptive data are almost always presented first before the testing of relationships in the data set.

In order to test or analyze variable relationships, two main branches of statistics are used in the social sciences. These are parametric and non-parametric. The former refers to a set of statistical tests based on the assumptions of normality (i.e., the normal curve). Typical parametric tests used in social research include the Student t-test (t), Pearson Correlation test (r), Analysis of Variance (ANOVA) and Regression (R^2). Conversely, non-parametric statistical tests do not hold the assumptions of normality (e.g., smaller samples and/or biased samples), which are not generalizable to normal populations. Typical non-parametric tests used here include McNemar's Test, Fishers' Exact Test, Mann-Whitney U, Kolmogorav-Smirnov (K-S) Test, and Wilcoxon Sign. One test used frequently by social researchers that cuts across both branches is the Chi Square Test (X^2) of Significance; however, different versions of it are used for both parametrics and non-parametrics. The three main issues about using any statistical test are (1) to examine the data and its assumptions, (2) to select the correct statistical test, and (3) to then interpret what it means.

Each parametric or non-parametric test used is presented as a test of significance. This lets you determine whether that test resulted in a statistically significant relationship between the variables (e.g., $p < .05$) or not (e.g., $p > .05$). As a result, students quickly find out that focusing on the significance levels of these inferential tests (when critiquing research studies) is far more important than the actual mathematical value of the text presented in the study (e.g., $X^2 = 14.32$). Because regardless of what statistical test is being used by the researchers, if it is not significant, it is not significant.

Figure 20 provides a list of criteria which can be used to critique the statistical data and tests used in the study.

Figure 20. Critiquing the Statistical Data and Tests Used

Statistical Criteria	Comments
1. Presentation	In which form(s) are the statistical data presented in the study?
2. Clarity	Are the statistical data presented clearly and understandably?
3. Descriptive Statistics	Which descriptive statistics are reported in the results?
4. Parametric Statistics	Which parametric statistical tests are used in the study?
5. Non-Parametric Statistics	Which non-parametric statistical tests are used in the study?
6. Statistical Significance	Are the findings of the inferential test(s) used (parametric or non-parametric) significant or not?

To summarize Figure 20, Box 19 lists the criteria for critiquing the statistical tests used in the study.

BOX 19: Critiquing the Statistical Data and Tests

Assess the study's statistical tests with respect to

- ✓ the form in which the statistical data is presented
- ✓ how clearly it is presented
- ✓ descriptive statistics used
- ✓ parametric statistical tests used
- ✓ non-parametric statistics used
- ✓ the significance of the statistical findings

Data About the Sample (n)

Although data describing the sample (n) typically occur in the Results section of the research study, they are sometimes presented in the Method section under the Sample Selection subheading. These data differ from how the sample was selected as they provide descriptive data about the sample that actually participated in the study. These data usually precede other descriptive data or statistical test data as they provide a context for understanding any subsequent findings. For instance, if the sample had an average age of 11.5 years old, it would make sense that it scored low on the Banking Skills Inventory Test. As a rule, the more detail presented about the peculiarities of the sample the better, as it assists in critiquing the findings yet to be presented. Sample data are either presented in narrative form (in the text if there is not excessive information) or in tabular form if there is more information about the sample.

Figure 21 and corresponding Box 20 present the criteria for analyzing the sample.

Figure 21. Critiquing the Sample (n) Data

Sample Criteria	Comments
1. Size	What are the final sample sizes in this study?
2. Bias/Representativeness	Would you say that this is a biased sample or a sample representative of a larger population?
3. Population (N) Bias	Is the population (N) from which this sample was selected biased itself?
4. Descriptive Factors	What does this sample actually look like?
5. Unique Features	Outside of its descriptive features noted above, does the sample have any other unique features as well (e.g. treatment contamination)?

Box 20 presents a summary of the criteria which should be considered when critiquing the sample data.

BOX 20: Critiquing the Sample (n) Data

Assess the study's sample data with respect to

- ✓ size of final sample
- ✓ biases or representativeness
- ✓ population bias
- ✓ descriptive factors
- ✓ unique factors

Discussion

Although this subheading may not actually appear in the Results section, it is important for any responsible researcher to now discuss their findings. Of all the subsections of the research report, the Discussion is where the researcher exercises his/her discretion on which "slant" to take, based on what is emphasized in this subsection. This is also deemed to be the most interpretive part of the research study as, quite literally, one researcher could discuss the finding of a "cup half empty" and render a conclusion. Yet another could discuss the same finding presenting the "cup half full" and render a very different conclusion. And technically, both interpretations and their corresponding discussions would be accurate.

Researchers normally discuss their results from two perspectives. One is from the perspective of the literature itself (i.e., did the findings support or refute the literature). The second is from the author's own perspective, analysis, or opinion, which is typically anchored in a point of view that is both logical (to the author) and/or "checkable." Ideally, a well-written discussion section should present a balanced (pro and con) and comprehensive explanation of the main findings of the study. Even though researchers are compelled to eventually render conclusions about their study findings, conclusions tend to have much more credibility if they are first discussed appropriately.

Figure 22 presents a list of criteria which may be used to critique the discussion part of the research study.

Figure 22. Critiquing the Discussion

Criteria	Comments
1. Relationship to the results	Does the discussion logically follow the previously presented results?
2. Emphasis	What findings from the results do the researchers primarily focus on in their discussion?
3. How were the results discussed?	How do the authors use literature to discuss their findings?
4. Balanced Review	Does the discussion present a pro and/or con view, or differing interpretations of the results?
5. Expected or not?	Were the results discussed expected by the researchers or not?

Corresponding Box 21 presents these criteria in list form.

BOX 21: Critiquing the Discussion

Assess the study's discussion with respect to

- ✓ its relationship to the results
- ✓ the emphasis
- ✓ use of literature in discussing findings
- ✓ whether it is a balanced review
- ✓ whether or not the results were expected

Limitations

Although rarely singled out as a separate subsection in a research study (except for academic theses or dissertations), responsible researchers will cite two to three limitations of their study, which in a sense temper their results and subsequent discussion of findings. Social research is, by its very nature, fraught with a degree of empirical uncertainty and obstacles (e.g., sampling, measurement, controlling for extraneous or confounding factors). As a result, good researchers negotiate the conduct of their studies around these existing and expected obstacles. If the researchers fail to cite some limitations, they give the appearance to the reader that they don't exist--and this simply is not true. Figure 23 cites the minimal criteria that should be used to assess study limitations.

Figure 23. Critiquing the Limitations of the Research Study

Criteria about Limitations	Comments
1. What are the limitations?	What study limitations are noted by the authors? What study limitations are not noted by the authors?
2. Major or Minor	Regardless of whether the limitations are cited or not, do you consider them to be major or minor limitations?
3. Future Research	What limitations need attending to in any future research studies of this nature?

Corresponding Box 22 summarizes these limitations.

BOX 22: Critiquing the Limitations

Assess the study's limitations with respect to

- ✓ what they are
- ✓ their significance (major or minor)
- ✓ future research needed

Implications

Congratulations! You have finally reached the final subsection of the research study. This is where the entire study comes together, as the authors relate their main study results or findings to particular groups who may benefit from them. Prior to assessing this, you first should understand that good social research ideally produces knowledge, first and foremost. So an appraisal of the types of knowledge which this study actually produced needs to be assessed here. A method for determining this has been developed and field-tested by Rosen, Proctor, and Staudt (1999). They present a hierarchy of knowledge on three levels, as indicated in Figure 24.

Figure 24. Types of Knowledge Derived from Social Research Studies

Knowledge Types	Definitions
1. Descriptive	Guides the classification of phenomena into meaningful conceptual categories (e.g., rates of poverty, prevalence of child abuse)
2. Exploratory	Guides the understanding of phenomena--their interrelationships, factors influencing their variability, and their consequences (e.g., relationship between depression and function, factors associated with hospital re-admission)
3. Control	Identifies means of influencing events or behaviors; the direction of influence can be maintenance (prevention) or change (intervention, increasing or decreasing). Examples include studies of prevention, demonstration of the effects of interventions, etc.

Note. Rosen, Proctor & Staudt (1999)

Using corresponding Box 23, you can now critique the main types of knowledge derived from the research study.

BOX 23: Critiquing the Main Types of Knowledge

What is the main type of knowledge found in this study?

    ✓ descriptive
    ✓ exploratory
    ✓ control

As indicated previously, it is incumbent for researchers to connect or relate their findings to a particular group of individuals who may potentially benefit from the study. Normally, one or two such groups or research beneficiaries are mentioned in this context. Figure 25 lists a number of such individuals, groups, or organizations that are really the study stakeholders, or those that may have a vested interest in the study.

Figure 25. A List of Potential Individuals, Groups, or Organizations Who are Typically Targeted in Social Research Study Implications

Potential Stakeholder Audiences	Comments
1. Study Participants	These are the individuals who provided the study data.
2. Other Consumers	Clients, patients, students, or other members of a general or treatment population.
3. Practitioners	Front-line practitioners who work in social, educational, health, legal, or human service agencies. These include governmental and non-governmental agencies.
4. Supervisors	Middle managers or supervisors working in social, educational, health, legal, and/or human service agencies.
5. Administrators	Upper level managers of social, educational, health, legal, and/or human service agencies.
6. Policy Makers	Persons involved in making policy decisions in social, educational, health, legal, and/or human service agencies.
7. Agency Boards	Boards of directors of social, educational, health, legal, and/or human service agencies.
8. Communities	Members of communities including individuals, groups, and organizations.
9. Program Planners	Persons involved in planning in social, educational, health, legal, and/or human service agencies.
10. Researchers	Other social researchers.
11. Educators	Those who may educate others about the findings of this study.
12. Funders	Individuals, groups, or organizations that provide funds for social, educational, health, legal, and/or human service agencies.
13. Providers of Authority	Individuals, groups, or organizations that provide legitimacy or authority for social, educational, health, legal, and/or human service agencies.
14. Other Organizations/ Agencies	Other governmental or non-governmental organizations or agencies not included in the list above.

Corresponding Box 24 lists the various research stakeholders who may benefit directly from the research study.

BOX 24: Critiquing the Implications

Toward which group(s) are the study's findings targeted?

- ✓ study participants
- ✓ other consumers
- ✓ practitioners
- ✓ supervisors
- ✓ administrators
- ✓ policy makers
- ✓ agency boards
- ✓ communities
- ✓ program planners
- ✓ researchers
- ✓ educators
- ✓ funders
- ✓ providers of authority
- ✓ other organizations/ agencies

9

Qualitative Social Research

> We don't see things as they are, we see them as we are.
> – Anais Nin

If you have been directed from the end of Chapter 3 to here, you probably have a study which is a qualitative research study. This chapter will help you to first determine this, and then provide you with the criteria to critique this study.

Although most of this text provides you with the tools to critique quantitative studies--as they represent the vast majority of published research in social science journals--qualitative research has recently (in about the last decade or so) gained considerable prominence in a number of disciplines namely social work, nursing, social psychology, sociology, business, education, music therapy, counseling, rehabilitation and business, to name a few.

Also, as indicated in Chapter 3, the method has not only regained popularity but also increased credibility as a bona fide "alternative" research method rather than the "other" research method (Holosko, 2001). Another trend has been the blending of both methods (qualitative and quantitative) successfully, complementing each other in the acquisition of knowledge. This has promoted an integration or interplay between these two methods (Cowger & Menon, 2001; Padgett, 1998; Strauss & Corbin, 1998).

Distinguishing Qualitative Methods from Qualitative Techniques

Students often get the issue of method and technique mixed up. Just because one uses qualitative techniques (e.g., in-depth interviewing, focus groups, observations), it does not necessarily mean that one is conducting a qualitative study. Yes, qualitative techniques do produce qualitative data, but qualitative research (as you will see) is embedded in a distinct set of methodological assumptions, and is very time consuming and comprehensive by its very nature. So please don't call a study qualitative just because it uses a qualitative technique or two.

Building on Chapter 3, an expanded definition of *qualitative social research is*

> *The study of people in their natural environments, as they go about their daily lives. It tries to understand how people live, how they talk and behave, and what captivates and distresses them. More importantly, it*

strives to understand the meaning peoples' words and behaviors have for them. (Tutty, Rothery & Grinnell, Jr., 1996, p.4)

As you note by the above definition, qualitative social research is a lot more involved than simply using a qualitative technique. In this regard, Figure 26 identifies five major criteria that must be present before a study can be deemed qualitative.

Figure 26. Necessary Elements of Qualitative Research Studies

Necessary Elements	Questions for Critiquing
1. Natural Environment	Does the study take place in a relatively natural setting or environment?
2. Absence of or Few Controlled Conditions	Are data collected without any or with few controls? Indeed, are they free-flowing observations of the phenomena of study?
3. Shared Experiences	Are the shared experiences of both the subjects and the researchers part of the study?
4. Different Observations/ Interactions With the Setting	Are there multiple and different observations/ interactions with the setting/individuals, or are there phenomena being studied which require flexible strategies?
5. Researcher as Participant	Is the researcher a true participant in the study?

Corresponding Box 25 summarizes these non-mutually exclusive elements of qualitative research.

BOX 25: Critiquing the Elements of Qualitative Studies

Does the study have all of the following:

- ✓ a natural environment
- ✓ absence of controlled conditions
- ✓ shared experiences
- ✓ different observations & interactions
- ✓ a participant researcher

If each element in Box 25 above received a checkmark, CONGRATULATIONS...You have found a qualitative research study to critique so

GO! Conversely, if any one of the above criteria in Box 25 did not receive a checkmark--

STOP! And go back to the literature/journals to find a study that satisfies all of these requirements.

Main Purposes of Qualitative Research

Every QL study has a main purpose. Some have both main and secondary purposes. However, if you read, reread, and critique the study carefully, it will have one of the main purposes listed in Figure 27, all of which are embedded in the methods of qualitative research.

Figure 27: Main Purposes of Qualitative Studies

Purposes	Comments/Explanations
1. Description	To describe phenomena, events, behaviors, activities, people, cultures, communities, or theories
2. Explanation	To explain phenomena, events, behaviors, activities, people, cultures, communities, or theories
3. Prediction	To predict phenomena, events, behaviors, activities, people, cultures, communities, or theories
4. Discovery	To discover phenomena, events, behaviors, activities, people, cultures, communities, or theories

Summary Box 26 allows you to check off and determine the main purpose of the QL study you are critiquing.

BOX 26: Main Purposes of Qualitative Research

Which of the following is the main purpose of the study you are critiquing?

- ✓ to describe
- ✓ to explain
- ✓ to predict
- ✓ to discover

Entering The Field

QL researchers use the term "field" as a short form for field setting. These are the actual sites where the collection of data took place. How a QL researcher entered the field and negotiated the setting is very important. Indeed, it affects how s/he comes to observe/study the phenomena and in turn, affects how s/he collects data on the phenomena of study. For example, not having permission to observe/study/collect data, being a stranger in the setting, and/or observing phenomena at the wrong time of day (or night) would all yield a totally different picture and, in turn, data set. As a result, entering the field is something that QL researchers take seriously. Figure 28 and corresponding Box 27 identify elements that should be considered and critiqued accordingly.

Figure 28: Entering the Field to Conduct Qualitative Research

Elements	Critique Questions
1. Casing the Setting	Does the researcher case the setting beforehand to determine its suitability or feasibility for study?
2. Permission Seeking	If the study involves entering a setting, examining secondary data like case records, observing people, or interviewing individuals/groups, etc., is permission (usually in the form of a letter or ethics consent form) sought by the researcher?
3. Obstacles/Restrictions	Are there any obstacles or restrictions, noted or not, by the researcher? How could these make it difficult for the researcher to enter the field?

BOX 27: Critiquing the Entry to the Field

Critique the following elements related to entering the field to conduct QL research

- ✓ casing the setting
- ✓ permission seeking
- ✓ obstacles/restrictions

How to Collect QL Data

Since QL research is normally conducted in naturalistic settings with relatively few controls, and the researcher's role is one of sharing these firsthand experiences, it is typical for QL researchers to use different and multiple data collection approaches as their studies unfold. These approaches can be broken down into four basic strategies as indicated in Figure 29.

Figure 29: Basic Qualitative Collection Strategies

Basic Strategies	Comments
1. Observation	Seeing, watching, or systematically observing normal/ abnormal events, situations, activities, behaviors, or phenomena.
2. Reading/Reviewing	Reading, reviewing, and then analyzing various materials (e.g., reports, records, files, studies, published/unpublished materials, personal documents, unobtrusive measure).
3. Interviewing	Conducting interviews with individuals, families, or groups of people.
4. Listening	Listening (with or without observing) and noting information heard from interactions in the setting.

As indicated in Figure 29, although these four basic strategies seem simple, they are not, as over the course of the QL study, the researcher may use any and all at different times during the course of the study. Box 28 summarizes these in simple checklist fashion.

BOX 28: Main Data Collection Strategies

Which of the following data collection strategies are used in the QL study you are critiquing?

- ✓ Observation
- ✓ Reading/reviewing
- ✓ Interviewing
- ✓ Listening

In each of the above data collection strategies (both Figure 29 and Box 28), the researcher's role can be very active or passive. This may vary accordingly, consistent with the needs of the study and data collection. You can plot any of the above data collection strategies, on the 4-point Likert type scale listed in Figure 30.

Figure 30: Continuum of Activity-Passivity of the QL Researcher's Role in Data Collection

1	2	3	4
Extremely Passive	**Somewhat Passive**	**Somewhat Active**	**Very Active**
Almost not visible in collecting the data	Visible but not intrusive in collecting the data	Being a part of the setting in collecting the data	Being a highly visible member of the setting in collecting the data

If you consider Figures 29, 30, and Box 28 together, you come to understand how varying degrees of involvement in data collection strategies come about (i.e., participant as observer vs. participant observer, reader/reviewer as compiler of data vs. reader/reviewer as data cross-referencer, casual interviewer vs. in-depth interviewer, and active listener vs. passive listener). The subtleties and distinctions between these various research roles are important to the collection of meaningful qualitative data.

Unfolding Assumptions/Questions Arising

As indicated earlier in this chapter (and also in Chapter 3) QL research involves a process that unfolds over time until the study is completed. Thus, the QL researcher turns the discovery stones on the beach over one by one as new ideas, assumptions, situations, events, issues, and questions unfold during the conduct of the study. Indeed, one of the purposes of QL research is to teach us to ask the right questions in an effort to formulate (data-based) hypotheses or grounded theory. Oftentimes, therefore, the ultimate purpose of the QL study may not become known until the very end of the study--and that is just fine for many QL researchers (although it may be frustrating for students critiquing their studies who expect a nice, neat purpose at the beginning of the study).

Figure 31 presents some ways that can be used to access this unfolding process related to the assumptions or questions of the QL study.

Figure 31: Unfolding Assumptions/Questions Arising

Issues	Critiquing Concerns
1. Stated or Not	Where and how are the study assumptions/questions stated?
2. Changing Nature	Do the assumptions/questions change as the study unfolds?
3. Unfolding Process	Can you identify why the assumptions/questions changed in the study (if they indeed changed)?
4. The Finale	What assumptions/questions are now clear as you read the completion of this study?

Box 29 summarizes the criteria listed in Figure 31, above.

BOX 29: Unfolding Assumptions/Questions Arising

Do the assumptions/questions of the study change according to

- ✓ whether they are stated or not?
- ✓ their changing nature?
- ✓ their unfolding nature?
- ✓ as you finish reading the entire study?

Time

The issue of both controlling time and spending time conducting research is a major concern for all social science researchers. It is of particular concern for QL researchers because often (1) they cannot control time variables, and (2) they investigate and collect data until they feel they have enough information to start their analysis. The latter is referred to as reaching a "data saturation" point, when collecting more data in the QL study basically won't add anything to what has been collected.

As a result, one of the challenges confronting QL researchers is allocating enough time for their investigations. This time consuming feature of QL research is a major reason why QL research is not appealing to many students, researchers, and/or funding bodies. In short, all QL research takes far more time than researchers imagine, and the inquiry process becomes one of perseverance, stamina, and strength of determination (and sometimes character) for many who conduct such studies. Figure 32 outlines issues which will help to assist in critiquing issues of time in QL research.

Figure 32: Time as a Factor in QL Research

Issues	Critiquing Questions
1. Length	How long did it take for this study to be conducted?
2. Controlled vs. Uncontrolled	How does the researcher both control and not control for time in this study?
3. Different Time Perspectives	Would sampling or data collection at different times than cited in the study change anything about its purpose, methods, findings, conclusions, or implications?
4. Reconciling Time	How does the researcher reconcile issues of time as they arise during the course of the study?

Corresponding Box 30 summarizes these time concerns.

BOX 30: Time Factors in QL Research

How do the researchers address the following issues related to time in the study?

- ✓ Length
- ✓ Controlled vs. uncontrolled
- ✓ Different time perspectives
- ✓ Reconciling time concerns

Sampling

In QL research, one may sample units from primary data sources (e.g., observations, interviews, surveys, focus group findings) or secondary data sources (e.g., census tract information, case files or records, annual reports of agencies, minutes from meetings). As stated, QL researchers rarely use a single entry point of one data set to conduct their studies. Typically, as the study unfolds, additional areas of inquiry branch out into different streams. This requires the researcher to paddle down the new stream, explore, and sample yet another perspective to gain more information about the phenomena they are studying.

Such multiple sample perspectives are a feature of QL research, which allow for rich experiential, contextual, or comparative data to be collected and then interpreted. QL researchers all believe that the more sampling perspectives the better, as more data can only yield more meaning to the phenomena of study (you can begin to see why QL studies take far more time than the researcher allots for).

Figure 33: Sampling Issues & Concerns for QL Research

Issues/Concerns	Critiquing Questions
1. Multiple Samples	What are the various primary and secondary sources used to collect the data in this study?
2. Biases	What biases exist in these samples and data?
3. Contextual Meaning	Are there enough data collected from these samples to provide a contextual meaning to the phenomena being studied?
4. Reconciling the Sample Issues	How does the researcher reconcile issues/concerns related to sampling in this study?

Corresponding Box 31 summarizes the issues/concerns related to sampling.

BOX 31: Sampling Issues/Concerns in QL Research

How do the researchers address the following sampling issues/concerns in the study?

- ✓ Multiple samples
- ✓ Bias
- ✓ Contextual meaning
- ✓ Reconciling sampling issues/concerns

QL Research Methods

Conducting QL research is not only time consuming and complex, but certain methods of QL research are in and of themselves both unique and require a special set of interpersonal and research skills. QL researchers, therefore, typically toss a "methods net" over their entire study, which gives the study a distinct methodological framework in which they can investigate their phenomena. Sometimes, however, multiple method nets are used in these naturalistic studies, as the quest to collect rich data requires a multi-method approach.

You should also know that numerous so-called qualitative methods texts have been written which describe these methodological paradigms from the standpoint of purpose, method, skill set, technology, values, and knowledge base. None of the main methods described here are a technique but are presented as an overarching or broader method. These are also the ones most frequently used by QL researchers. As indicated earlier, students often get the notion of QL technique and method mixed-up a bit. Indeed, one may be using a qualitative technique to collect qualitative data (e.g., interviewing or observing), but the use of such techniques does not mean that one is conducting a qualitative study. The latter incorporates the distinct use of one of the overarching QL methods described in Figure 34. Figure 34 presents rather simplified definitions of these main qualitative methods.

Figure 34: Defining the Main QL Methods

QL Method	Simplified Definitions
1. Phenomenology	To describe and understand the lived experiences of individuals.
2. Narration	Detailed narrative accounts of individuals, events, themes, life histories, and their meanings.
3. Case Study	Examining individual units comprising cases of individuals, groups, families, settings, interventions, communities, or cultures.
4. Ethnography	Studying cultures to learn about their interactions, values, meanings, behaviors, language, interactions, meaning, and/or worldview.
5. Action/Participatory Research	Identifies a social problem or concern and seeks information about them by collaborations with individuals and/or organizations.
6. Participant Observation	Observing activities, events, people, interactions, meaning, and/or worldview through the cultivation of personal relationships.
7. Grounded Theory	The systematic generation of data based theory to develop explanations, hypotheses, concepts, typologies, meanings, and/or descriptions of phenomena.
8. Practice/Program Evaluations	To assess and understand practice/program goals, objectives, and/or outcomes using naturalistic inquiry methods.

Note. These are written as "bare bones" definitions of these methods and in no way attempt to minimize their complexity. All of the above main qualitative methods seek answers to the questions about the what, how, or why of a phenomenon, then explore, rather than measure or test, aspects of it.

So by using Figure 34 and corresponding Box 32, you can determine the main method used in the qualitative study.

> BOX 32: Main QL Research Methods
>
> Which of the following describe the main QL research method of the study you are critiquing?
>
> - ✓ phenomenology
> - ✓ narration
> - ✓ case studies
> - ✓ ethnography
> - ✓ action/participatory research
> - ✓ participant observation
> - ✓ grounded theory
> - ✓ practice/program evaluation

Qualitative Research Techniques

After determining the main QL method of the study you are critiquing, it is important now to determine which of the various QL research techniques are used in collecting the study data. Figure 35 describes the main techniques used by QL researchers.

Figure 35: Main QL Research Techniques

QL Techniques	Comments
1. Observations	Through observational schedules, charts, maps, inventories, random occurrences, field notes, audio/visual recordings, etc.
2. In-Depth Interviews	Using structured, semi-structured, or open-ended interviews. These may include using standardized or non- standardized questions, measure scales, etc.
3. Log Books/Case Notes/ Field Books/Diaries	Recording information in the form of chronological events in field books, log books, case notes, or diaries. These may include pictorial, printed, or audio/visual notations.
4. Unobtrusive Measures	Using non-reactive measures in which the researchers and subjects do not necessarily directly interact with each other. These may be recorded before, during, and after the fact in the study.
5. Historical Accounts	Using historical information to research the phenomena of study.

Figure 35. continued

QL Techniques	Comments
6. Secondary Accounts	Using secondary accounts both collected in formal ways (e.g., census tract data, literature, clinical files), and less formal ways (e.g., rough notes of key informants, technical or unpublished reports, correspondence, e-mails).
7. Focus Groups	Organized discussions with selected individuals to gain information about a topic.

As you can see from the above, any and all of these main techniques may be used by the QL researcher. The corresponding Box 33 summarizes these QL techniques.

BOX 33: Main QL Research Techniques

Which of the following QL techniques are used in the study?

- ✓ observations
- ✓ interviews
- ✓ log books/case notes/field books/diaries
- ✓ unobtrusive measures
- ✓ historical accounts
- ✓ secondary accounts
- ✓ focus groups

Critiquing Methods and Techniques Together

As indicated earlier, students sometimes have difficulty in separating QL methods from techniques. In order to better understand this relationship, it is easier to first identify all of the QL techniques used in the study and then determine which major method (or two) they collectively fall under. Please note that the majority of QL studies will have only one major method; however, a few may have two. None will have more than two method nets which overarch their entire studies.

Table 4 combines Figures 34/35 and Boxes 32/33 and allows you to use the grid to check off the various QL techniques and main methods of the study you are critiquing.

Table 4: Assessing the QL Techniques and Main Methods of the Study

Main Methods	Main Qualitative Techniques						
	Observations	In-Depth Interviews	Log Books Field Books Case Notes Diaries	Unobtrusive Measures	Historical Accounts	Secondary Accounts	Focus Groups
Phenomenology							
Narration							
Case Studies							
Ethnography							
Action/ Participatory Research							
Participant Observation							
Grounded Theory							
Practice/ Program Evaluation							

QL Data → Categories → Themes

QL researchers transform their data, often collected both in large amounts and from multiple sources, into eventual numerical or conceptual categories. These categories then become transformed into themes, hence the transitional subtitle: QL data → categories → themes. Data collection stops after the QL researchers feel they have exhausted or saturated the phenomena they are studying.

In the past decade or so, some excellent computer software programs have been developed to help with the task of transforming data → categories → themes. Some of the better known programs are NUD.IST through Sage Publications (www.sagepub.com); ATLAS/ti through Scientific Software Development (www.atlasdi.de); The Ethnograph by Qualis Research

Associates (www.qualisresearch.com); and WordStat (www.simstat.com/wordstat.htm). If you are interested in learning more about these and other software programs, see Padgett (1998), Weitzman and Miles (1995), and/or the suggested additional resources list at the end of the primer.

Basically raw data becomes transformed into something called "partially processed data" as a preliminary step before categories/codes called "meaning units" are then developed. The final stage involves transforming these into themes and, in many cases, grounded theory.

Figure 36 and corresponding Box 34 define how data become transformed in such studies. In critiquing the QL study, you need to pinpoint where in this transformation process the data are being analyzed and interpreted, or in short, their meaning.

Figure 36: Transformation of QL Data into Meaning

Data Forms	Comments/Critique Questions
1. Raw Data	Identify all of the raw data forms in the study. How were they collected?
2. Partially Processed Data	What does the data look like in its partially processed form? How were these data processed?
3. Categories/Codes	What are the main categories/codes of the data collected in the study?
4. Themes	Identify all major and minor themes of the data.
5. Grounded Theory	Do the authors transform their data into grounded theory? If "yes," what does the theory help to explain? If "no," could you use their themes to develop a grounded theory?

BOX 34: Transforming QL Data Into Meaning

Identify the following in the study:

- ✓ raw data
- ✓ partially processed data
- ✓ categories/codes
- ✓ themes
- ✓ grounded theory

Checking the Rigor of QL Research by Using the 3 Rs

QL studies can be assessed for their rigor by using the simple 3-R Test. This test assesses the reactivity, researcher biases, and respondent biases (Lincoln & Guba, 1985).

Their simplified definitions are presented in Table 5.

Table 5: Assessing the Rigor of QL Studies by Using the 3 Rs

Criteria	Simplified Definitions & Critique Questions
1. Reactivity	This refers to how much the setting is reacting to the researcher. Do the authors interfere with the setting in ways to change its natural state, behaviors, events, feelings, or activities?
2. Researcher Biases	This refers to the slant/perspective or biases the researchers may have in their studies. Identify how researcher biases influence the study.
3. Respondent Biases	This refers to whether the subjects of the study had certain biases that may have affected the method or findings of the study. Identify how respondent biases influence the study.

BOX 35: Using the 3 Rs to Assess Rigor in QL Studies

Does the study have

- ✓ reactivity
- ✓ researcher biases
- ✓ respondent biases

10

Concluding Remarks

Nothing in life is to be feared. It is only to be understood.
– Marie Curie

By using this primer and the website critiquing template systematically, students or consumers of social research can basically pick up any published research study and critique it piece by piece, section by section, subheading by subheading, from the title at the beginning to the reference list at the end. It is assumed that such critiquing skills will not only make you a better and more informed consumer of social research, but will also eventually make you a better producer of research. As well, repeated use of this skill will help you to appraise social research in a more critical way, that is, with an acknowledgement of its precise strengths and limitations, and with a more tempered skeptical--not cynical--mind's eye. It is only through developing a more open-minded and critical perspective that consumers of social research can advance their learning of research.

Upon using this text, you also have to be reminded of a few other things. One is that social science research, by its very nature, is fraught with empirical uncertainty. Researchers constantly struggle with issues of how to better ask the right questions, sample more selectively, measure variables more precisely, analyze their data more completely, and disseminate their findings to groups who can best benefit from their investigations. Such realities are viewed as the nature of the research business, and in no way should they inhibit striving for good research, or that research which is well-written. It is only through our commitment to good research that new facts, theories, insights, phenomena, and knowledge can be advanced.

Upon using the text, you may have some questions, concerns, or insights that you wish to share. I have set up a website to both include your questions/concerns/insights and respond to them personally. Hopefully, you and others will benefit from our shared dialogue, and I look forward to hearing from you as you use this text. The website address is http://counseling. wadsworth.com/Holosko1e. You may also download from the website the critiquing template made up of text boxes contained in the primer. These will allow you to cut and paste parts of articles into the template and critique them according to the various criteria in each subsection. The critiquing template is designed to present summaries of selected criteria used to evaluate various sections and subsections of a social research study. Finally, I have included in the appendix a summary of all the critiquing criteria from each chapter so you can have this information at your fingertips. I wish you well in becoming better critical thinkers and astute consumers of social research, and I leave you with the words of Aristotle:

It is a mark of the educated man and a proof of his culture that in every subject he looks for only so much precision as its nature permits.

Appendix A
Critiquing a Social
Research Study

The following represents a list of questions and/or criteria to be used in critiquing a social research study. Also listed are the chapters in the text where you can go to identify these criteria/questions. They are also separated according to whether the study is quantitative or qualitative.

Critiquing a Social Research Study	Chapters	
	Quantitative	Qualitative
1. Does the study meet the scientific requirements?	2	2
2. Is it a research study?	2	2
3. Is it a quantitative study?	3	3
4. Is it a qualitative study?	9	9
5. Is it clearly written?	4	4
6. Assess its title.	4	4
7. Assess the authors' affiliations.	4	4
8. Assess the abstract	4	4
9. Assess the references.	4	4
10. Is there a centrality of purpose between the introduction, method, and results?	5	5+9
11. Critique the Introduction according to:		
• the literature review	6	6+9
• study purpose	6	6+9
12. Critique the Method according to		
• the sample selection	7	7+9
• the study design	7	9
• classification type	7	9
• data collection procedures	7	9
• design objectives	7	9
• design parameters	7	9
• number of groups	7	9
• researcher's role	7	9
• the issue of time	7	9
• materials/instruments used	7	7+9
13. Critique the Results according to		
• findings	8	8+9
• tables, graphs or charts	8	8+9
• statistical data and tests used	8	8+9
• sample (n) data	8	9
• discussion	8	8+9
• limitations	8	8+9
• implications	8	8+9

Appendix B
APA Resources &
Suggested Readings

Additional APA Resources

The manual itself is available through
    The American Psychological Association
    Order Department
    P.O. Box 92984
    Washington, D.C., 20090-2984
    Telephone (202) 336-5510 or 1-800-374-2721
    Fax (202) 336-5502,
    www.apa.org, or order@apa.org.

A.P.A. - Style Helper (2000) www.apa.org/apa-style

Suggested Additional Readings on Using Computer Software in QL Research

Padgett (1998, p. 151) offers a list of recommended readings if you would like to gain more information on using computer software programs to analyze QL data. These are:

Fielding, N.G, & Lee, R.M (Eds). (1991). *Using computers in qualitative research.* London: Sage Publications.

Hesse-Biber, S., Dupuis, P., & Kinder, T. S. (1991). HyperRESEARCH: A computer program for the analysis of qualitative data with an emphasis on hypothesis testing ad multimedia analysis. *Qualitative Sociology, 14,* 289-306.

Miles, M. B., & Weitzman, E. A. (1995). Computer programs for qualitative data analysis. In M. B. Miles & A. M. Hubberman (Eds.), *Qualitative data analysis: An expanded sourcebook* (pp. 311-317). Thousand Oaks, CA: Sage

Muhr, T. (1991). ATLAS/ti: A prototype for the support of text interpretation. *Qualitative Sociology*, 14, 349-371.

Pfaffenberger, B. (1998). *Microcomputer applications in qualitative research*. Newbury Park, CA: Sage Publications.

Richards, T.J., & Richards, L. (1994). Using computers in qualitative research. In N. K. Denzin & Y. S. Lincoln (Eds.), *Handbook of qualitative research, 2nd Edition*. (pp. 445-462). Thousand Oaks, CA: Sage Publications.

Seidel, J. V., & Clark, J. A. (1984). The Ethnograph: A computer program for the analysis of qualitative research. *Qualitative Sociology*, 7, 110-125.

Tesch, R. (1990). *Qualitative Research: Analysis types and software tools*. New York: Falmer.

Tesch, R. (Ed.). (1991). Computers and qualitative data. *Qualitative Sociology*, 13(3 & 4) [Special issues, Parts 1 and 2].

Weitzman, E. A., & Miles, M. B. (1995). *Computer programs for qualitative data analysis*. Thousand Oaks, CA: Sage Publications.

References

American Psychological Association. (2001). *Publication manual of the American Psychological Association* (5th ed.). Washington, DC: Author.

Bloom, M., Fischer, J. & Orme, J. (1999). *Evaluating practice: guidelines for the accountable professional.* Boston: Allyn & Bacon.

Campbell, D. & Stanley, J. (1963). *Experimental and quasi-experimental designs for research.* Chicago: Rand McNally.

Cone, J. & Foster, S. (1993). *Dissertations and theses from start to finish: Psychology and related fields.* Hyattsville, MD: APA Publications.

Cowger, C. & Menon, G. (2001). Integrating qualitative and quantitative research methods. In B.A. Thyer (Ed.), *Handbook of social work research methods* (pp. 473-485). Thousand Oaks, CA: Sage Publications.

Filstead, W.J. (1970). *Qualitative methodology: Firsthand involvement with the social world.* Chicago: Markham.

Gelfund, H. and Walker, C. (2000). *Mastering APA style: Student's workbook and training guide* (2nd ed.). Hyattsville, MD: APA Publications.

Grinnell Jr., R. (2001). *Social work research & evaluation* (6th ed.). Itasca, IL: F. E. Peacock.

Grinnell, Jr., R. and Unrau, Y. (2005). *Social work research and evaluation: Quantitative and qualitative approaches* (7th ed.). New York: Oxford University Press.

Holosko, M.J. & Holosko, D. A. (1999). What have we learned from articles published in the Family Preservation Journal? *Family Preservation Journal*, (4)1, 1-12.

Holosko, M.J. & Leslie, D. (1997). Obstacles to conducting empirically-based practice. In J. Wodarski & B. Thyer (Eds.), *Handbook of empirical social work practice, Volume 2: Social problems and practice issues* (pp. 433-451). New York: J. Wiley & Sons, Inc.

Holosko, M.J. (2001). An overview of qualitative methods. In B. Thyer (Ed.), *Handbook of social work research methods* (pp. 263-273). Thousand Oaks, CA: Sage Publications.

Padgett, D.K. (1998). *Qualitative methods in social work research: Challenges and rewards.* Thousand Oaks, CA: Sage Publications.

Rosen, A., Proctor, E. & Staudt, M. (1999). Social work research and the quest for effective practice. *Social Work Research*, 23, 4-14.

Schatzman, L., & Strauss, A. (1973). *Field research: Strategies for a natural society.* Englewood Cliffs, NJ: Prentice Hall.

Strauss, A. & Corbin, J. (1998). *Basics of qualitative research* (2nd ed.). Thousand Oaks, CA: Sage Publications.

Szuchman, L. & Thomlison. B. (2004). *Writing with style: APA style for social work* (2nd ed.). Belmont, CA: Brooks/Cole-Wadsworth.

Thyer, B. A. (2001). *Handbook of social work research methods.* Thousand Oaks, CA: Sage Publications.

Tripodi, T., Fellin, P. & Meyer, H. (1983). *The assessment of social research* (2nd ed.). Itasca, IL: F. E. Peacock.

Tutty, L., Rothery, M., & Grinnell, Jr., R. (1996). *Qualitative research for social workers.* Boston: Allyn & Bacon.

Weitzman E.A. & Miles, M.B. (1995). *Computer Programs for Qualitative Data Analyis.* Thousand Oaks, CA: Sage Publications.